C0-DKM-725

Want 3 more books for FREE?

As a special thank you for downloading this book we would like to give you
3 MORE books absolutely FREE!

Scroll to end of this book to find out how!

Fun Learning Facts About Black Holes

All Rights Reserved. No part of this
publication may be reproduced in any form or
by any means, including scanning,
photocopying, or otherwise without prior
written permission of the copyright holder.
Copyright © 2014

WHAT ARE BLACK HOLES?

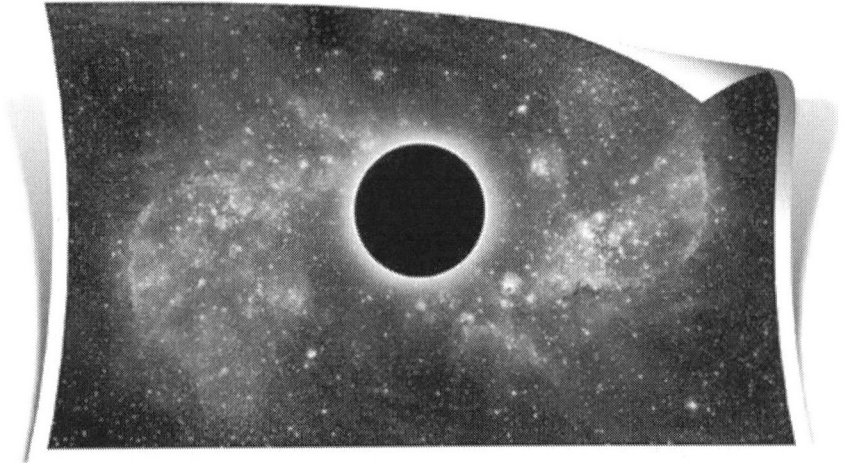

Black holes are what are left behind when a big star runs out of fuel. Usually when a star runs out of fuel it turns into a White Dwarf, or Neutron Star. However, when a huge star 10 or 15 times as big as our sun runs out of fuel, it goes through a process called Supernova. This is when a star goes through a huge explosion, scattering all the parts of the star around the universe, apart from a cold central part, which becomes a black hole.

WHY IS IT CALLED A BLACK HOLE?

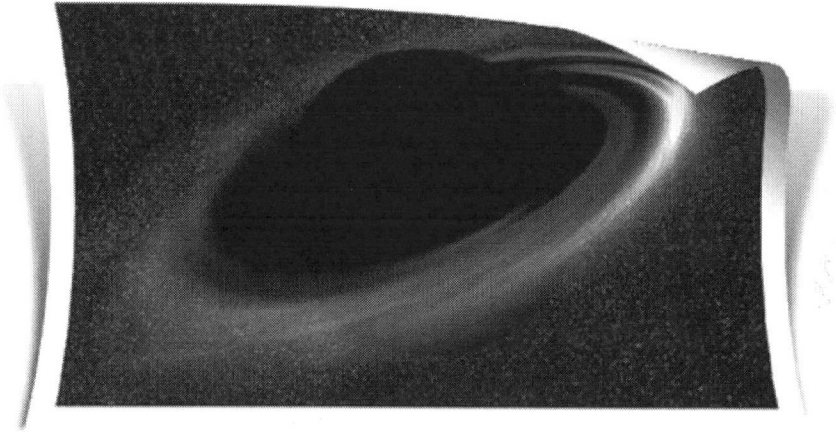

Black holes get their name from their appearance. black holes are areas with very, very high gravity. In fact, their gravity is so strong that nothing can escape from it, not even light. This means that when you look at a black hole, it is completely black, since there is no light that is able to escape from it. This is where they get their name.

HOW BIG IS A BLACK HOLE?

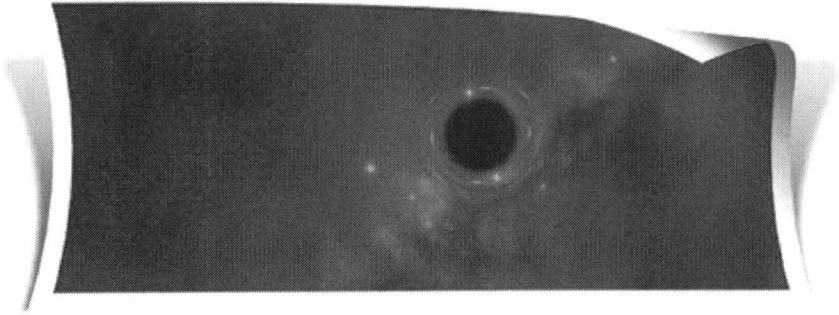

Black holes can be a number of sizes. They grow and grow for a long time, which means that the size of a black hole can change a lot from the next black hole. The biggest black hole we know of was found 2 years ago, and has a mass equivalent of 17 BILLION suns! Luckily, its 250 million light years away from Earth, so we don't have anything to worry about!

WHERE IS THE CLOSEST BLACK HOLE?

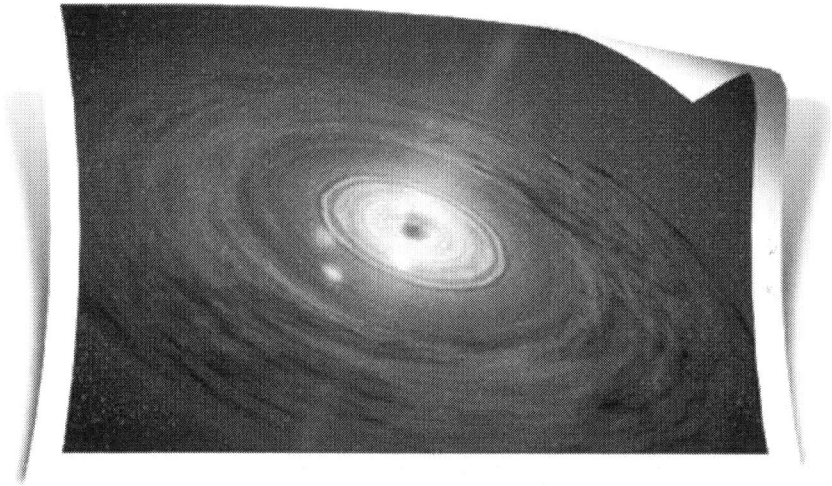

The closest black hole to Earth is known as V4641 Sagittarii. This is the closest black hole to Earth. At one point, it was believed to be only 1,600 light years away, however scientists later discovered that this measurement was inaccurate. In actual fact, V4641 Sagittarii is more like 24,000 light years away.

HOW HEAVY IS A BLACK HOLE?

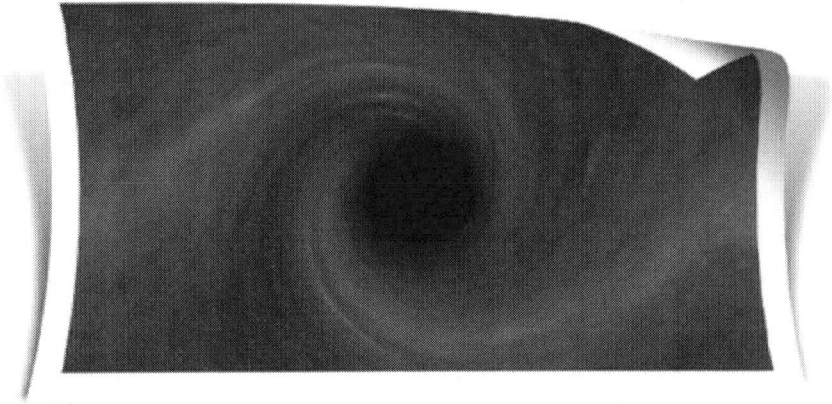

Black holes have an incredibly high amount of mass. Black holes are formed when stars collapse into tiny little points, but maintain all of their original mass and weight. Because of this, a black hole can have the total mass of around 10 to 30 billion times the mass of the Sun. All of this incredible mass is contained within the single point which lies at the center of a black hole. The huge mass contained within such a tiny area is what gives black holes such an incredible gravitational pull.

WHAT IS AN EVENT HORIZON?

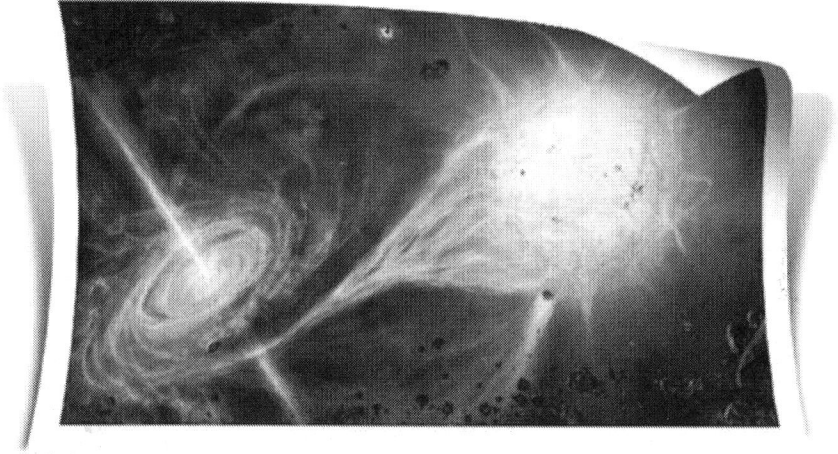

The event horizon is the border on a black hole between being able to escape, and not being able to escape. As you get closer and closer to a black hole, the gravity gets stronger and stronger. So, there is a point where the gravity becomes so strong that nothing can ever escape once it has gone past this point. That point is known as the event horizon. If you were to fly into a black hole, after you had gone past the event horizon you would never be able to escape, no matter how fast your spaceship was.

HOW LONG DO BLACK HOLES LAST?

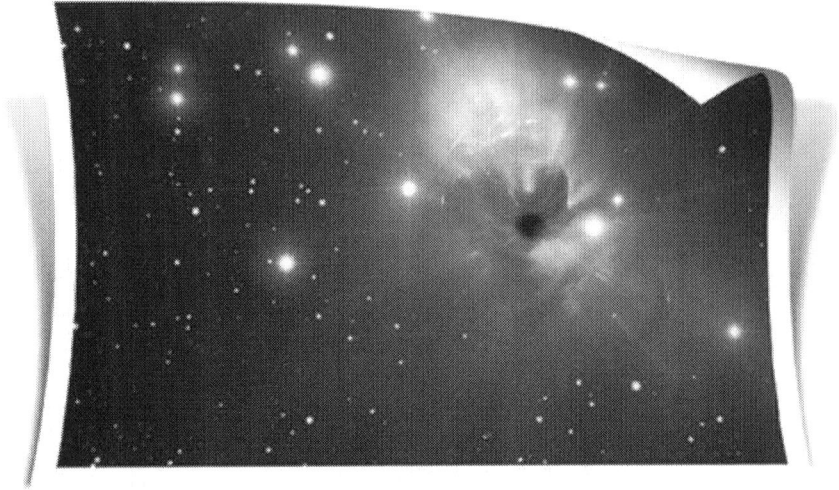

A very, very long time. In fact, for most of our history, we have believed that black holes last forever. Famous physicist Steven Hawking was able to figure out that black holes are slowly losing radiation, which over a long enough time will cause them to run out of energy and disappear. However, the current huge black holes that are in the universe today will take so long to run out of energy that it is insignificant. They will essentially be around forever.

WHAT HAPPENS IF I GO INTO A BLACK HOLE?

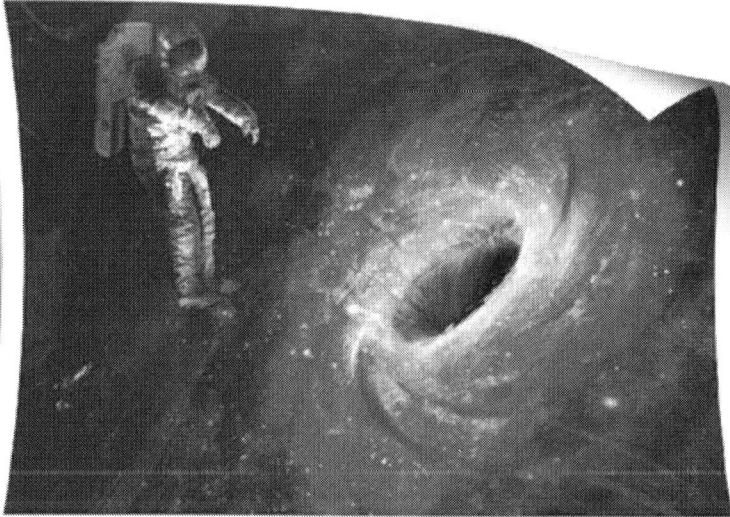

You would die VERY quickly. While I definitely don't advise going into a black hole, there is something interesting that would happen. As the gravitational forces being exerted on you get stronger, you would feel your head and feet be stretched, while your sides are pushed together. This process is known as 'spaghettification' by scientists, since it will leave you long and thin, like a strand of spaghetti!

HOW DO SCIENTISTS FIND BLACK HOLES?

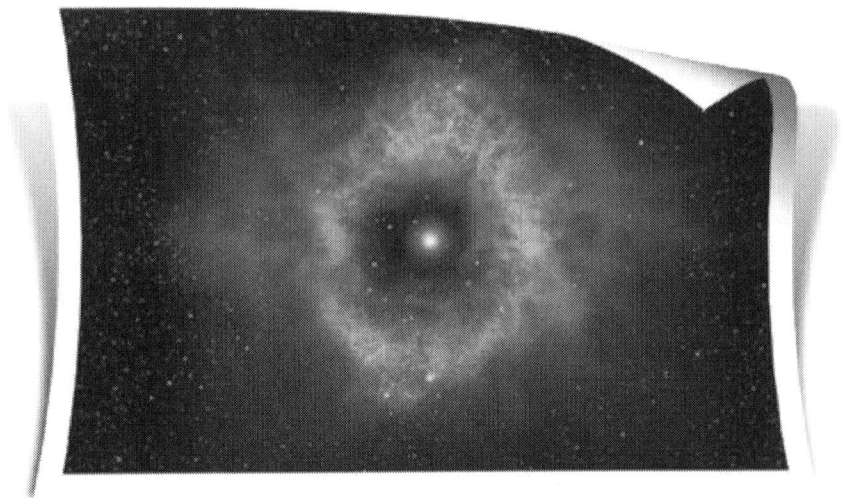

Black holes are hard to see by scientists, since no light ever escapes from them. Scientists only are able to see black holes by examining the stars that give off light near to a black hole. The light coming from these black holes gets warped by the black hole, and scientists are able to detect this. This is the only way that we know of to find a black hole, since you can't see the light that they give off.

WHAT DOES A BLACK HOLE LOOK LIKE?

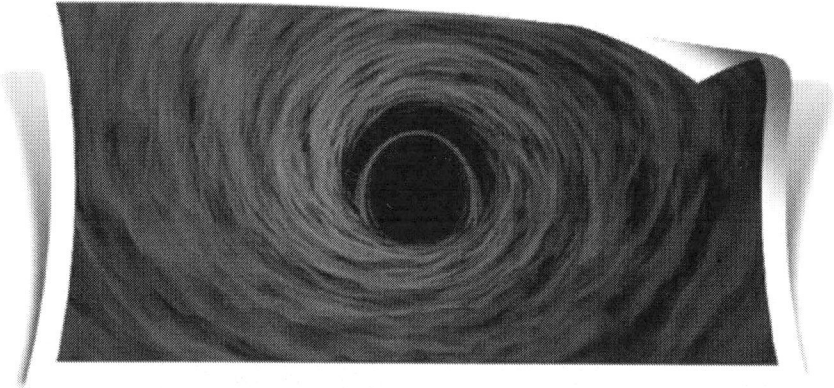

Black holes look like big, black holes! Because light can't escape from them, they just look like holes in space where there is nothing. Many illustrations of black holes depict them as funnel-shaped, but in actual fact they are more like spheres. The gravity that black holes exert spreads out in all directions, which means that they are spherical in all directions.

DO BLACK HOLES MOVE?

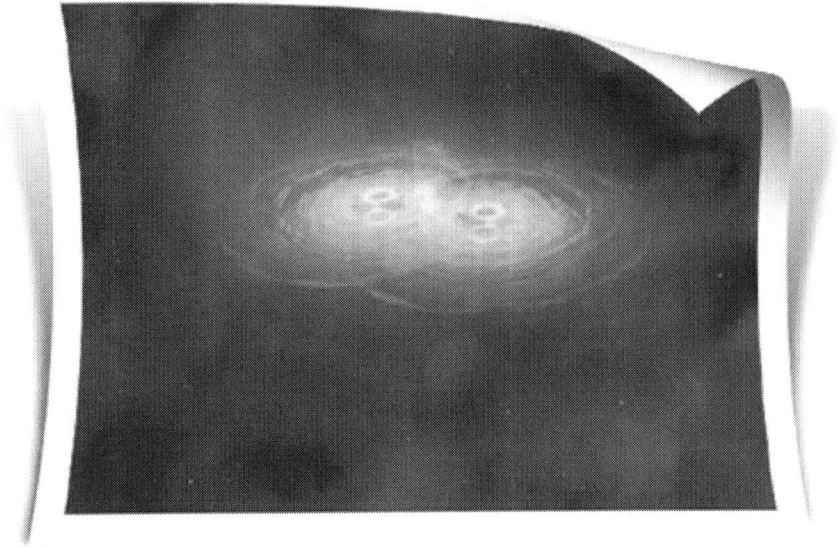

Yes! When a black hole is formed, the star that is collapsing starts to rotate. As the star collapses, this rotation speeds up, and is able to keep going while the star goes through supernova. The black hole that is created keeps this spinning motion, which means that a lot of black holes spin around. However, black holes do not move apart from spinning around.

WHAT EFFECTS DO BLACK HOLES HAVE ON TIME AND SPACE?

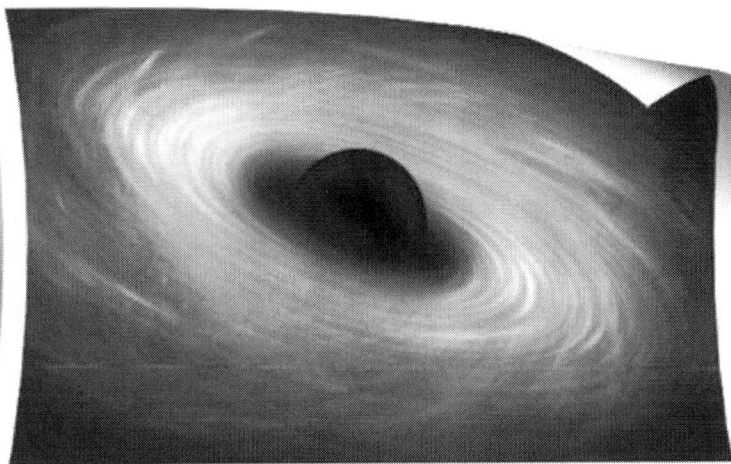

Black holes do a lot of strange things because of their incredibly strong gravity. They are able to distort space, making gravity curve around them. In addition, due to their high gravity, they are able to slow down time. In a black hole, time moves slower. In fact, as you get closer and closer to the centre of a black hole, time slows down to an incredibly slow pace.

CAN YOU TRAVEL THROUGH TIME IN A BLACK HOLE?

There are currently some theories about how to time travel using a black hole. A scientist called Roy Kerr proposed a theory which would use special kinds of rotating black holes called Kerr holes to travel through time. Because of the special way these black holes rotate, they would not have incredibly strong gravity, which means that you would be able to pass through them and potentially warp through space and time.

WHO DISCOVERED BLACK HOLES?

While Albert Einstein is credited with reinvigorating the scientific community about black holes, a scientist named John Mitchell was the first person to come up with the idea. He theorised about an area of gravity that was so strong that light could not escape, back in 1783. Albert Einstein was able to "rediscover" black holes in 1916 when he published his theory of gravity.

WHAT SOUND DO BLACK HOLES MAKE?

While light can easily travel through space, sound can't. This is because sound waves are unable to move through the vacuum of space. However, if we were able to hear a black hole, it would make a very crackling, static-y sound. This sound comes from the high speeds that particles go through when they enter a black hole and move past the event horizon. So while black holes are quiet, they would be making a very crackly sound, similar to a television which has no antenna.

WHAT IS A WHITE HOLE?

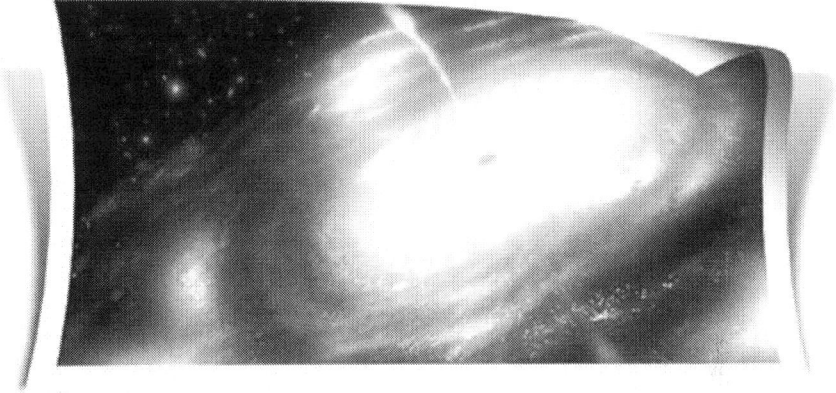

A while hole is the opposite of a black hole, which so far has not been proven to exist, but is theorised by scientists. If something entered a black hole, it would exit through a white hole. While we so far have no proof that white holes exist, there are various theories which discuss them. For example, in Roy Kerr's time travel theory, after you enter into a black hole to travel through time or space, you would have to exit through a corresponding white hole.

WHERE ARE BLACK HOLES USUALLY FOUND?

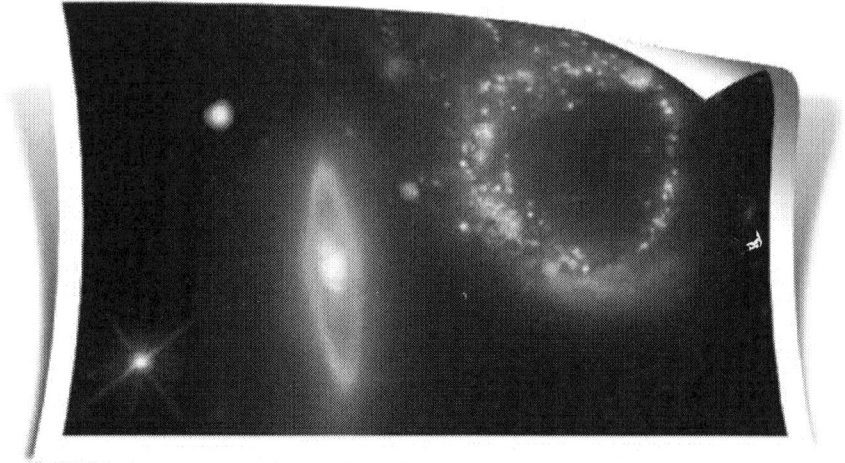

Lots of galaxies have black holes at the center of the galaxy. These kinds of galaxies are known as Active galactic nuclei. Our galaxy, the Milky Way, is one of these galaxies. The Milky Way has a huge black hole, known as a supermassive black hole, at the center of it, around 25,000 light years from Earth.

ARE BLACK HOLES USUALLY BY THEMSELVES?

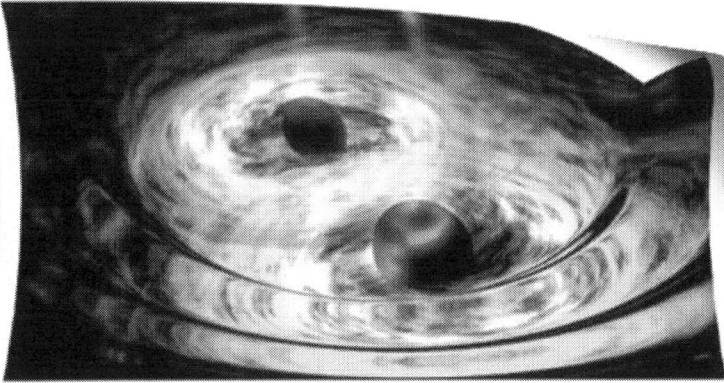

While most black holes suck in everything around them, to be completely alone, sometimes black holes can pair up in a phenomenon known as double black holes. Double black holes are formed when two galaxies collide with each other, causing both of their centres to form black holes which orbit each other. The two black holes orbit each other at an incredibly high speed, around 4,000 km per second!

ARE BLACK HOLES ALL THE SAME?

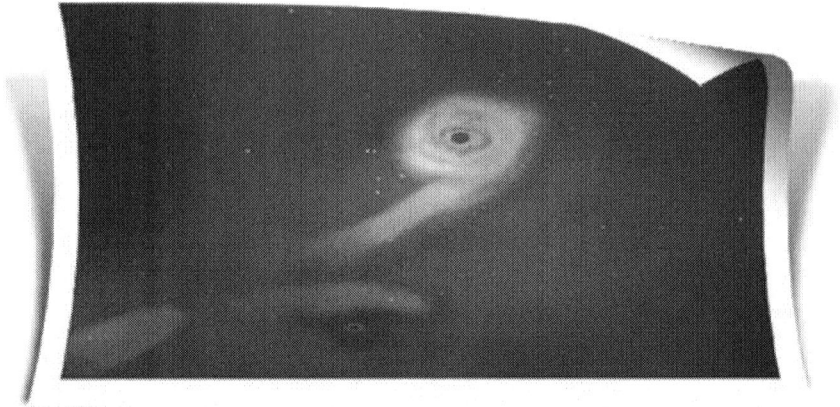

No. There are actually multiple different types of black holes. There are spinning black holes, which are formed by their stars having lots of rotation when they collapse, and non-spinning black holes. In addition, there are electrical black holes which have electric charge. Electrical black holes can also be spinning, to create spinning electrical black holes. There is a lot about black holes that we don't yet know, and there may even be other types that we haven't discovered yet!

CAN ONLY STARS BECOME BLACK HOLES?

All the black holes that we know of so far have been formed by stars collapsing into a single point. However, in the future it is possible that anything can become a black hole. If an orange, for example, collapsed so that all of its mass was contained within a single point, it would become a tiny version of a black hole. In this way, anything can become a black hole if its mass collapses down to a single point.

Thank You!

We hope you enjoyed the book! All pictures and words were lovingly put together by experts who really love what they do! We really hope you learned something new today!

We would really appreciate it, if you could PLEASE take the time to let us know how we're doing by leaving a review on the Amazon website. We appreciate any comments you may have – what you enjoyed about the book, what additions you would have liked to have seen and what you would like to see in future publications.

Any comments will help understand better what you and your kids most enjoy and allows us to better provide exactly what you want!

Thought Junction Publishing

A NOTE FROM THE AUTHOR

Please, Please leave an honest review...

It really helps me out a lot, if you could leave an honest review on the book you have just read, and it takes only a few seconds to do so!

Here's a direct link to your orders page so you can quickly review the book

Click here - http://amzn.to/1omG5V2

Thank you SO much in advance for helping me!

You can find more of my books here -

http://amzn.to/1qEnx3l

READ MORE OF MY BOOKS

Here's just a small selection of my books -

Get the above titles and more here:
http://amzn.to/1qEnx3l

Claim Your 3 FREE Books!

Thank you for reading this book - we truly appreciate your interest, reviews and feedback! It gives us the motivation to keep publishing new books that inspire and educate people around the world!

As a special thank you, we would like to give you 3 Free Books!

Here's how to claim yours:

1) Leave a review on this book - We love hearing your kind words!
2) Once you have left your review, get your free books here:

>> http://ebookrebel.com/3freebooks <<

60854465R00017

Made in the USA
Lexington, KY
21 February 2017